LET'S VISIT SOUTHEAST ASIA

by John C. Caldwell

LET'S VISIT AMERICANS OVERSEAS
LET'S VISIT ARGENTINA
LET'S VISIT AUSTRALIA
LET'S VISIT BRAZIL
LET'S VISIT CANADA
LET'S VISIT CENTRAL AMERICA
LET'S VISIT CHILE
LET'S VISIT CHINA
LET'S VISIT COLOMBIA
LET'S VISIT FORMOSA
LET'S VISIT FRANCE (with Bernard Newman)
LET'S VISIT INDIA
LET'S VISIT JAPAN
LET'S VISIT KOREA (with Elsie F. Caldwell)
LET'S VISIT MEXICO
LET'S VISIT MIDDLE AFRICA
LET'S VISIT THE MIDDLE EAST
LET'S VISIT NEW ZEALAND
LET'S VISIT PAKISTAN
LET'S VISIT PERU
LET'S VISIT THE PHILIPPINES
LET'S VISIT SCOTLAND (with Angus MacVicar)
LET'S VISIT SOUTHEAST ASIA
LET'S VISIT THE SOUTH PACIFIC
LET'S VISIT VENEZUELA
LET'S VISIT VIETNAM
LET'S VISIT WEST AFRICA
LET'S VISIT THE WEST INDIES

Let's Visit Southeast Asia

Hong Kong to Indonesia

John C. Caldwell

The John Day Company, New York

Contents

Why Southeast Asia Is Important 8
Geography and Climate 10
Southeast Asia — Long Ago 13
Invaders from the North 16
Coming of the Europeans 17
The British-Related Nations and Colonies 25
  Hong Kong 25
  Federation of Malaysia 33
    Malaya 38
    Sarawak and Sabah 44
    Brunei 49
    The Government of Malaysia 50
  Singapore 51
The Republic of Indonesia 56
The Buddhist Nations of Southeast Asia 64
  Thailand, or Siam 65
  The Kingdom of Cambodia 75
  Laos, Land of a Million Elephants 81
The "Chinese" Nations 84
  North and South Vietnam 84
Index 96

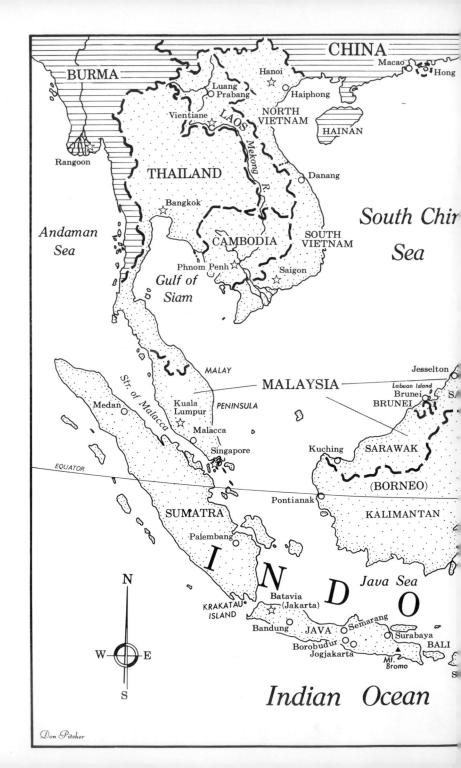

SOUTHEAST
ASIA

0   100   200   300   400   500
Scale of Miles

ezon City

PHILIPPINES

Pacific Ocean

es Sea

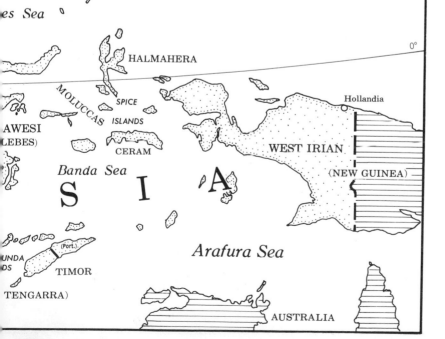

HALMAHERA

0°

MOLUCCAS

SPICE

ISLANDS

Hollandia

AWESI
LEBES)

CERAM

WEST IRIAN

(NEW GUINEA)

Banda Sea

S   I   A

Arafura Sea

UNDA
DS

(Port.)

TIMOR

TENGARRA)

AUSTRALIA

Why Southeast Asia Is Important

It was not many years ago that names like Saigon, Bangkok, and Singapore meant nothing to most Americans, but today these places are often in the news. If for no other reason, Southeast Asia is important because of the war in Vietnam. This book is being written in 1966, and at this time there are over 300,000 American soldiers, marines, airmen, and sailors fighting in South Vietnam. Even if this war should end quickly and peace should come in Vietnam, the country will remain very important to us.

For even after the fighting is ended, the United States will probably be busy for years in helping rebuild South Vietnam. Our country is already giving economic help to South Vietnam, Laos, and Thailand. Hundreds of Peace Corps members are at work in Thailand and Malaysia. Peace Corps workers will probably be going to Indonesia soon. And during the last few years the United States has become involved in Southeast Asian affairs in other ways. There is an organization called the Southeast Asia Treaty Organization, or SEATO for short, to which our country belongs. SEATO is somewhat like NATO in Europe, a banding together of free world nations to protect one another in case of Communist attack.

Southeast Asia might be called the rice bowl of Asia. In this part of the world, rice is grown in such large amounts

Southeast Asia is the rice bowl of Asia.

that it can be exported. By this we mean that the rice can be sold to other nations.

Communist China, with its huge population, has not been able to solve its food problem. Most Chinese like rice as the main part of every meal. Communist China has not been able to raise enough rice to feed its people. For this reason, the Communists would like very much to gain control of Vietnam and especially of Thailand. We shall read more about this interesting country in another part of this book.

Southeast Asia is rich in other resources, in addition to rice. Malaysia is one of the great tin-producing nations of the world, with almost one-third of all the tin produced in the world coming from this country. Malaysia and other areas are also rich in natural rubber, or the rubber which comes from trees. We shall learn about rubber plantations in another part of the book.

Spices — pepper, nutmeg, cinnamon, and cloves — are grown in several countries. Later we shall read how Southeast Asia was first visited by European sea captains in search of spices. Finally, there are rich deposits of oil on two of the islands that are situated off the southern tip of Asia.

So we can understand that Southeast Asia is important in many ways. In this book we are going to learn about countries or political divisions of Southeast Asia, with a population of almost 190,000,000. Our country is pledged to defend several of the nations in Southeast Asia. We have been involved in a very costly war in this part of the world. Because of its great wealth of resources, Southeast Asia is of importance to the Communist world.

This is one of the world's most interesting areas, and as we go along, we shall learn more about each country in Southeast Asia.

Geography and Climate

Look at the map of Southeast Asia. You will see that it is a long peninsula, with a big bulge in the middle and near the top. You might say that it looks like a giant nutcracker. The area we are to visit begins at the border of China and extends south for 1,500 miles. There are hundreds of islands off the southern tip of the peninsula, which is called the Malay Peninsula.

In the big fat bulge, Southeast Asia is about 750 miles wide, but if you were visiting the Malay Peninsula at its narrowest point and were in an airplane, you could see a part of the Indian Ocean and the Gulf of Siam (a part of the Pacific Ocean) at the same time. This narrow place is called the Kra Isthmus, and it is only 30 miles across.

Before we visit the different countries, let's learn more about the whole area. Much of Southeast Asia is covered with jungles, swamps, and mountains. In the jungles and mountains there are tigers, wild elephants, monkeys, and even an animal called the wild cow. But there are also great modern cities, some of them founded a little more than 100 years ago. There are also the ruins of great cities and temples, built

There are tigers in Cambodia, Laos and Vietnam.   USIS

hundreds of years ago. And there are vast areas of rich farm-land.

Four of the nations we are going to visit are ruled by kings, although in one of these the king is elected and has no authority. Two areas are British colonies, and two others are independent nations, members of the British family of nations called the Commonwealth. One country is a republic like the United States, and one country is a dictatorship. The tenth and last country we shall visit in this book is the world's fifth largest in population, a republic governed by army generals.

All Southeast Asia lies within the tropics. This means that the weather is usually very hot and humid. The equator passes between the big city of Singapore and Jakarta, the capital of Indonesia. Southeast Asia is subject to monsoon weather. By this we mean that there is a time of the year when sudden rains drench the area. Sometimes the rain continues for several days. The monsoon period is somewhat different in different countries. In Thailand the heavy rains usually come from the end of May to the middle of September. On the east coast of the Malay Peninsula the monsoon period is from October to February. In Singapore, at the very tip of the long Malay Peninsula, November and December are the wettest time of the year. During the monsoon period the rainfall is very heavy, and the weather is humid and sticky. There are parts of Indonesia where 240 inches of rain fall each year. So we may think of this part of the world as generally hot, rather wet, and humid.

We should also mention that in the northern parts of Southeast Asia there are big storms called typhoons. A typhoon is very much like a hurricane in the Atlantic. We know that hurricanes sometimes strike Florida and other states along the Atlantic coast. A typhoon has very high winds and very heavy rainfall. The typhoon season is usually from midsummer through September.

Now that we know something of the geography and climate and about the importance of Southeast Asia, we shall learn something of its history.

Southeast Asia – Long Ago

The history of Southeast Asia is exciting and interesting. In a way, it was the crossroads of Asia, with many people moving from Central Asia into Southeast Asia and some of them eventually moving on into the islands of the South Pacific. There were and are sultans and sheiks, pirates, and ancient kingdoms.

Even before people from other areas began to visit Southeast Asia, men were living in this area. Archaeologists, the people who dig in the ground for ancient cities and fossils, have found bones of the earliest men there. So we might say that in this part of the world there was an aborigine population. The word "aborigine" means the original people, such as the American Indians, who were already living in the Americas when the Europeans arrived.

The first people to come to Southeast Asia were from Central Asia. These people established their civilization thousands of years ago. Some of them stayed on, and others moved farther to the east and south. There are thousands of islands from the southern tip of the Malay Peninsula to near the coast of Australia. Over the centuries people from Southeast Asia moved through these islands until eventually they populated the islands of the South Pacific. There were Melanesians, who now live in islands such as the Fiji Islands, and Polynesians, who eventually got as far as New Zealand, Tahiti, and many other island groups. In fact, we find a relationship between these migrations and our state of Hawaii. The Polynesians who came to Hawaii arrived from the islands now called French Polynesia. Since many of these people had no written records, we can only guess about these great migrations of the past.

If you look at a map of Asia, you will see that in order to get from India to China, ships must sail around the tip of the Malay Peninsula. Because of this fact of geography, Southeast Asia became a water crossroads. Centuries ago, traders, sailors, and pirates visited Southeast Asia on their way to and from other parts of the continent. The history of all the countries has been influenced by these visitors of many years ago. Of great importance to the history and religions of Southeast Asia is the beginning of visits from India, even before the time of Christ. Some of the people from India came by boat and settled the Malay Peninsula or in the Indonesian islands. Still others came overland, following the coastline of the peninsula. These travelers sometimes continued overland, across the narrow peninsula, and settled in the big bulge that we can see on the map.

The Indians brought their religions, called Hinduism and Buddhism, and their written language, called Sanskrit. Nearly 2,000 years ago there was a powerful Hindu kingdom, called Funan, which existed in the part of Southeast Asia we now call Cambodia. And in Vietnam there are ancient ruins showing the evidence of Indian settlements and religions there many many centuries ago. Because of the visitors from India, there are still about 60,000,000 persons in Southeast Asia who follow the religion called Buddhism.

Many centuries after the Indians brought their way of life, a new people arrived. They had traveled all the way from the Middle East by way of India. These were the Arabs, and they came in their small ships, called dhows, to buy the wonderful spices of Southeast Asia. It is possible that the Arabs had some seacoast settlements 2,000 years ago, but it was not until about 100 years before Columbus discovered America that they began to have great influence.

In 1403, Arabs conquered and settled around the city of Malacca, near the southern tip of the Malay Peninsula. The strait separating the peninsula from the islands of the south is very narrow. The warlike Arabs were able to control the strait from the big port they built in Malacca. They spread from this city all through Malaya and into the islands south of Malaya.

As the Arab traders and armies moved about, they took their religion with them. The Arab people are, for the most part, followers of Mohammed, and their religion is called Islam, or Mohammedanism. We speak of Mohammedan people as Moslems (sometimes spelled Muslims). To this day most of the Malay people who live in the Malay Peninsula and in the hundreds of islands to the south practice this religion. In some areas where the people were either Buddhist or Hindu, the change was soon made to the Moslem religion.

Invaders from the North

In addition to the Indians and Arabs, there were other people who came to Southeast Asia, and these came from the north. Two thousand years ago China was a powerful nation. At that time there were many small countries in Southeast Asia. Many of the small nations paid tribute to the powerful emperors of China. As far back as 111 B.C., China ruled parts of the region. And just as the Indians and Arabs brought their religions and customs, so did the Chinese. As we read about the various countries of Southeast Asia, we shall learn that millions of Chinese live there now. There are also many people there who have been influenced by the Chinese.

Now we may begin to see why we call Southeast Asia the crossroads of the continent. By knowing about the Arabs, Indians, and Chinese, we can sort out the countries of Southeast Asia and put them in groups. Let us do it this way: First, there are the Mohammedan, or Moslem, people, including all the Malays who live in the Malay Peninsula and on the islands to the south.

Next, there are the Buddhist people, living in the northern and western parts. These people became Buddhist because of the influence of India many centuries ago.

Finally, there are the people who came under the influence of the Chinese. For the most part they live in the northern and eastern sections of Southeast Asia. Since Buddhism also traveled from India into China and from China back south, many of these people, too, call themselves Buddhist.

But before we begin to put all the people and countries into groups, we must know about other visitors who came to Southeast Asia. They came from much farther away and were originally looking for spices.

Coming of the Europeans

Remember that our own country was settled by people who sailed across the Atlantic Ocean. They came from Britain, France, Spain, and some of the smaller countries of Europe. Soon after the time that Europeans began sailing west across the Atlantic, they began exploring in the other direction. The Arab and Indian traders had sent spices from Southeast Asia to India and the Arab countries. By caravan or by boat the spices reached the Middle East and, finally, Europe.

It is hard for us to realize that people could get terribly

excited about pepper, nutmeg, or cinnamon. But the only flavorings the people of Europe had for their food were salt and a few herbs. The spices from Southeast Asia changed the history of the world. The traders and the sea captains of the Continent soon began to send their ships in search of spices. Some, like Columbus, tried to find a short cut by sailing across the Atlantic. Some sailed on, through the Strait of Magellan and across the Pacific. Others sailed around the tip of Africa, then across the Indian Ocean to Southern and Southeast Asia.

In a way we owe something to this part of the world. North America was discovered by men like Columbus looking for a shorter way to the Spice Islands. In time, Europeans came to all parts of Southeast Asia and had a great deal of influence on the history of this area.

We have already seen that Malacca on the Malay Peninsula was conquered by Arabs in the early fifteenth century. The story of this one city tells us much about the activities of European countries in Southeast Asia. In 1511, Malacca was conquered by the Portuguese and held by them for a long period. In time, this city was held by the Dutch, the French, and the English. Finally, the English traded the city, which controlled the Strait of Malacca, for the Dutch-held island of Sumatra. In other words, the English and the Dutch simply swapped their possessions.

The Europeans fought the sultans and the pirates and also

spent a great deal of time fighting one another. The main interest at first was to find the islands from which the spices had come. Two great trading companies were established to develop the land conquered by the Europeans in Southeast Asia. The East India Company was established in England in 1600; the United East India Company, in Holland in 1602. In time these two big companies had their own armies and actually ruled large areas of Asia for their governments in Europe.

Slowly the European nations began to gobble up the little countries of Southeast Asia. The many small kingdoms of the area fought among themselves, too, and often a weak kingdom would ask one of the European nations for protection. Some parts of Southeast Asia voluntarily came under European rule.

By the middle of the nineteenth century the British controlled all of what is now India and Pakistan, all of Malaya, and part of the big island of Borneo. Farther to the north they acquired Hong Kong, a naval base and trading center on the coast of South China.

The Dutch took most of the islands south of Malaya and for many years fought with the British over Malaya. The French captured the big bulge in the peninsula of Southeast Asia and established a large colony, known as Indochina. This colony extended all the way from the border of China to the Gulf of Siam.

The Portuguese conquered large areas but could not hold

them. They were very cruel in their rule and either lost their holdings through local uprisings or were driven out by the other European nations. The Spanish did not acquire any part of Southeast Asia. Magellan reached the Philippine Islands, and soon after, this archipelago of more than 7,000 islands was controlled by Spain.

Of all the nations in Southeast Asia only one remained free and independent. Siam, as Thailand was then called, was a large and strong country. We shall read later how this big country was able to avoid being gobbled up by the Europeans.

This was the situation until the end of World War II, when European nations either voluntarily gave up their colonies or were driven out by people who wanted to be free and independent. The French and Dutch no longer control any colonies in Southeast Asia. The Portuguese still hold part of an island in the Indonesian Archipelago and a tiny colony on the coast of China, called Macao. In 1960 the British gave independence to Malaya, which, however, remains in the British Commonwealth of Nations. Great Britain still has other colonies in Southeast Asia, and this fact gives us another convenient way to group the people and the countries of the area. Let us do it this way:

First, we shall read about the places and countries that are still under the control of Great Britain and about other countries which are independent members of the British family of nations. For instance, the Federation of Malaysia is in the second group. It is an independent member of the

British Commonwealth of Nations. The Federation of Malaysia includes eleven states on the Malay Peninsula (formerly called Malaya) and Sarawak and North Borneo (now called Sabah). All these used to be British colonies. Hong Kong, on the coast of South China, is still a British colony, and Brunei is a small British protectorate and colony, on the island of Borneo. Singapore is an independent city-state and is also a member of the British family of nations. We shall include the colony of Hong Kong in our visit to Southeast Asia because it is the gateway through which most travelers pass to reach Southeast Asia.

After Hong Kong, we shall visit Indonesia, formerly a colony of the Netherlands and now an independent nation. Ninety percent of Indonesia's people are Moslems.

Next, we shall visit the free nations whose people still

There are many Buddhists. These Cambodian boys are young monks.

USIS

practice the Buddhist religion as they have done ever since the time when settlers from India arrived in their lands. These are Thailand (Siam) and the kingdoms of Cambodia and Laos.

Finally, we shall read about the two nations in Southeast Asia which were most influenced by Chinese visitors centuries ago. These are the Republic of South Vietnam and the Communist Democratic Republic of North Vietnam. Many of the people in these two countries are also Buddhist, but in most ways, their customs and lives have been influenced by the Chinese.

This is a convenient way to divide the countries we are to visit. But we must remember one other fact. At first the Chinese were visitors, but during the past two centuries many thousands of Chinese have settled in Southeast Asia. In some places there are more Chinese than native people. In Singapore, 80 percent of the population is Chinese. Nearly half the people of Malaysia are Chinese. But the original inhabitants of both Singapore and Malaysia are Malays, now belonging to the Moslem religion. There are also many Chinese living in Thailand and, in fact, in almost all the nations of Southeast Asia. It certainly is mixed up, isn't it? Chinese living in a Mohammedan country, independent but under the protection of the British queen! That is the way we could describe Singapore.

All the countries of Southeast Asia have some things in common. The weather is hot and wet. There are jungle-covered mountains and some flat areas or swamps along the rivers and seacoast. With the exception of Malaysia, no country has good transportation systems. In many areas, either there are no highways, or the roads may be open only during the dry seasons.

Rice is the main food of all the people of Southeast Asia. It is grown wherever there is flat land and plenty of water.

Although there are new and modern cities, there are also many primitive areas and many small villages. There are automobiles and trucks and buses, but the people of Southeast Asia also use other means of transportation. The pedicab is found in all countries. This vehicle is a descendant of the rickshaw. Instead of being pulled by a man on foot, a pedicab is pulled or pushed by a man riding a bicycle attached to the cab.

Now we shall begin our visit to the nations of Southeast

Flooded rice fields ready for planting. AID

Asia by reading about the British-related nations, starting with the British crown colony of Hong Kong, a great bustling city on the coast of South China.

THE COUNTRIES OF SOUTHEAST ASIA

BRITISH-RELATED COUNTRIES

Hong Kong	British crown colony	Population, more than 4,000,000
Malaysia	Independent federation of former British colonies	Population, 9,000,000
Singapore	Independent city-state, former British colony	Population, 1,900,000
Brunei	Small British protectorate on island of Borneo	Population, 100,000

THE REPUBLIC OF INDONESIA

	Independent, former Dutch colony	Population, 105,000,000

THE BUDDHIST NATIONS

Thailand	Constitutional monarchy. Bangkok is the capital.	Population, 30,000,000
Cambodia	Constitutional monarchy, former French colony. Pnompenh is the capital.	Population, 6,000,000
Laos	Constitutional monarchy, former French colony. Vientiane is business capital; Luang Probang, where king lives, is spiritual capital.	Population, probably about 2,000,000

THE "CHINESE" NATIONS

South Vietnam	Independent republic, formerly part of French Indochina. Saigon is the capital.	Population, 17,000,000
North Vietnam	A Communist people's republic, formerly part of French Indochina. Hanoi is the capital.	Population, 16,000,000

The British-Related Nations and Colonies

HONG KONG

Until 1913, China was ruled by emperors who did not like outsiders in their country. European traders were not allowed to settle or establish trading posts in China. In 1839, Great Britain went to war with China in order to force the Chinese to open their country to European trade. Great Britain won the war, and in 1841 a rocky, hilly island was ceded to the British.

The name of the island was Hong Kong, which means Fragrant Harbor in Chinese. Hong Kong has become one of the most important and interesting cities in the world. When the British took possession more than 100 years ago, it was inhabited by a few fishermen. Now this British colony has a population of more than 4,000,000. It is Asia's greatest trading center and has one of the best harbors in the world.

In 1860, after another war with China, the British took possession of a 3½-square-mile peninsula on the mainland across the harbor from Hong Kong Island. This part of the colony of Hong Kong is called Kowloon, which means Nine Dragons. In 1898, Great Britain decided that it needed more land. A large area on the mainland and almost seventy-five small islands nearby were leased or rented to the British for ninety-nine years. This part of the colony is called the New Territories. The map on page 26 shows us Hong Kong Island, Kowloon, and the New Territories. The total area is 391 square miles.

Map of Hong Kong.

Hong Kong's harbor is one of the best in the world.

CAT

The main government offices are on Hong Kong Island, in a section called Victoria. We could call this the capital of the colony. Most of the population lives in and around Victoria or in Kowloon. The highest point on Hong Kong Island is 1,823 feet in elevation and is called Victoria Peak. Notice the picture of the harbor, taken from the peak. It is this beautiful protected harbor, covering 17 square miles, that has made Hong Kong so important.

In addition to Victoria Peak, there are other mountains, some almost 3,000 feet high. Where there are no mountains, there are hills. When new buildings go up, it is necessary first to cut off the top of a hill.

The climate of Hong Kong is subtropical. This means that it is rather warm and humid. The rainy season is from May to August. And beginning in the late summer there are frequent storms called typhoons. This is the name given to hurricanes in the Orient. There are high winds and much rain with typhoons. One of Hong Kong's problems is that many people live on hillsides. During typhoons the heavy rains cause landslides, and people are often killed.

Hong Kong's fine harbor is visited by ships from all over the world. The colony has become important and very popular with American tourists for another reason. It is a free port. This means that there are no taxes or customs duties collected on most goods. Because of this, it is possible to buy many things in Hong Kong for much less money than any place else in the world. Watches, typewriters, cameras, and clothing are a few of the things that can be bought at bargain prices.

In recent years Hong Kong has become a manufacturing center. Textiles and plastics are most important. But Hong Kong has become especially famous for its clothing and tailors. The finest British cloth is brought to Hong Kong. A man or a lady may be measured in the morning and have a finished suit by the same evening! Hong Kong tailors are not only fast, but also good and inexpensive.

American tourists like to visit Hong Kong, not only because they can get clothing or make other purchases, but also because it is an unusual city. We could say that the Western world and the Orient meet in this city. There are wide streets and modern buildings; there are also narrow alleys like the one shown on page 30. Notice the laundry hanging out to dry.

On page 30 there is a picture of Chinese boats. These boats are in a typhoon shelter, an area protected by a sea wall so that small boats can ride out a storm. It is interesting to know that 150,000 persons live out their lives on boats. Whole families live and die, perhaps go to school or visit a medical clinic, on boats. The small boats, like those in the foreground of the picture, are called sampans. The large boats with sails are called junks. Chinese fishing junks often sail hundreds of miles in search of fish. In the second century after Christ, Chinese junks are known to have visited the Persian Gulf!

Ninety-nine percent of the population of Hong Kong is Chinese. Most of the foreign or non-Chinese population is British. There are also many American businessmen and numerous Portuguese citizens.

The map on page 26 shows us another reason why Hong Kong is important. The part of the colony known as the New Territories borders on Communist China. Hundreds of thousands of Chinese have been able to gain freedom because of Hong Kong's location. No one knows the exact number of refugees from China, but more than 2,000,000 persons have crossed the border into the New Territories. Some refugees come by land, others by boat; many thousands have crossed into the nearby Portuguese colony of Macao.

The stories of the refugees are sometimes thrilling, sometimes sad. Men have left their families, hoping somehow to send back for them. Some people have floated for miles on inner tubes to reach the waters of Hong Kong. Many people have been killed by Communist guards as they tried to cross to freedom. The border is heavily guarded; there are rows of barbed wire fences. Yet the people still come out, seeking the freedom they cannot find in China.

Because of the refugees, Hong Kong is a terribly crowded city. Some refugees live on the tops of roofs; others build shanty towns on the hillsides. The British government has tried to help by building many resettlement estates where refugees may live by paying very low rent. There is a picture

Chinese junks and sampans.

A narrow and crowded Hong Kong street.

of a resettlement estate on page 32. Each room is usually nine feet by twelve feet. There is a community bathroom and kitchen on each floor. Often there is a school and small play area on the roof. I have visited rooms in resettlement estates where as many as twenty persons live. The people must sleep in shifts — that is, while one-half of the people sleep, the others must be out of the room until it is their turn to use the sleeping space.

The refugees have caused many problems. It has not been possible to provide schools and teachers for all the children. Education is not compulsory, and it is not free. It is thought that at least 100,000 boys and girls do not attend school. Often a family with several children has money to educate only one. It must be a hard decision to select the one child (almost always a boy) who is to go to school.

Hong Kong is too small in area to have big rivers. For years, rainwater, which was held in reservoirs, was the only water supply. People were allowed water for perhaps one hour every three days. Now there are big pipe lines to Communist China. The British government must buy its water from China.

Because of the refugees, there are not enough schools or teachers, not enough doctors or hospitals, not enough good paying jobs. And as we have said, until recently there was not enough water. Also, 90 percent of Hong Kong's food must be bought from China.

Hong Kong is not independent, but it is free. There is

This is a refugee resettlement building.

freedom of speech, religion, the press. The colony is governed by a representative of the queen of England. The governor is advised by an executive council and a legislative council. Since Great Britain has diplomatic relations with Communist China, there are numerous Chinese Communists in Hong Kong. There are Communist newspapers, banks, and stores.

Like West Berlin, Hong Kong is an island of freedom almost surrounded by the Communists. And it is important as the gateway to Southeast Asia. We have mentioned the busy harbor; the airport is one of the world's busiest, too. All the important cities of Southeast Asia are within a few hours of Hong Kong by way of modern jet planes. Each day there are many flights to Saigon, Manila, Bangkok,

Singapore. So let us pretend that we have boarded a big airliner for a visit to other British-related parts of Southeast Asia. Our first stop will be the independent nation called Malaysia.

FEDERATION OF MALAYSIA

This is a good place for us to learn the meanings of the words "Malay," "Malayan," "Malaysia," and "Malaya." The word "Malay" is usually used as a noun. We speak of the Malays, or the Malay people. The Malays are the brown branch of the human family. We know there are white, yellow, black, red, and brown people. The Malays inhabit the Malay Peninsula, the islands of Indonesia, and the Philippines. The word "Malayan" is an adjective. We speak of a Malayan village or Malayan food. The word "Malaysia" has come into use only in recent years. This word was invented to describe the country that was formed when the former British colonies on the Malay Peninsula and Borneo became independent. Finally, the word "Malaya" is the name of that part of Malaysia on the Malay Peninsula.

For Malaysia is a divided country, one part separated from the rest by 400 miles of the South China Sea, which is part of the Pacific Ocean. The mainland part, or Malaya, covers almost 51,000 square miles. Sarawak and Sabah are on the big island of Borneo, part of which belongs to Indonesia. Sarawak has an area of 48,250 square miles; Sabah has an area of 29,388 square miles. The total area of the

Federation of Malaysia is 128,440 square miles, and it has a population of more than 9,000,000.

There are eleven racial groups in the population. About 40 percent is Malay; 33 percent, Chinese; 10 percent, Tamil (from Southern India). There are pygmy Negritos and other aborigine tribespeople, including Dyaks, Dusuns, and Kayans. Some of the tribespeople wear little clothing, still hunt with blowguns, and poisoned darts.

Before we read about the history of this part of Southeast Asia, let us recall why Malaysia is important. It is by far the largest producer in the world of raw or natural rubber. This is rubber which comes from the rubber tree. About one-third of the world's tin comes from the Malay Peninsula. And each year almost $10,000,000 worth of black pepper is produced, mostly in Sarawak on Borneo. Because of these and other resources, Malaysia is the most prosperous nation in Southeast Asia.

We have learned that Arabs settled in the city of Malacca on the coast of the Malay Peninsula in 1403. Soon all the people of the peninsula were Moslems.* But although the people had one religion, they had many governments. The Malay Peninsula was divided into many separate states, each ruled by a sultan or raja. The rajas and sultans fought among themselves. From time to time foreign invaders also came to Malaya.

* For a detailed description of the Moslem religion, see John C. Caldwell, *Let's Visit the Middle East,* rev. ed., (New York, The John Day Co., 1966).

Malacca was invaded by the Portuguese in 1511; then the Dutch drove the Portuguese away; the British took Malacca away from the Dutch, who held the city until 1818. Then, in 1824, the British traded the whole island of Sumatra for Malacca.

While the Dutch and British were fighting for power in Malaya, it was also being attacked by a people called the Bugis. They were a warlike seagoing people from Borneo and other islands south of Malaya, some even coming from the Philippines. All through the eighteenth century the Bugis invaded Malaya, and Bugi chiefs became sultans of several Malayan states. As if all this were not enough, the powerful kingdom of Siam to the north often sent invading armies into Malaya.

The sultans of Malaya had a difficult time. For many years there was a custom of sending tribute to powerful neighboring countries so that the big neighbors would not attack. The tribute was an ornamental plant, called the *Bunga Mas,* with leaves and flowers of gold and silver. The sultans and rajas of the Malay Peninsula were always sending *Bunga Mas* to someone. Sometimes these Malay chiefs sent the tribute to Siam; then Siam, afraid of *her* powerful neighbor, would send the *Bunga Mas* to China!

It was Great Britain which finally brought peace to Malaya. Much of the credit goes to one man, Sir Stamford Raffles. We shall read more about this unusual Englishman, who founded the city of Singapore.

As we have seen, the British had control of Malacca from time to time. In 1786 they had acquired Penang, an island close to the west coast of Malaya. The British East India Company hoped to make Penang into a great trading city. But it was too far north to control the narrow strait between the tip of the Malay Peninsula and the big island of Sumatra. Control of the strait was very important, for all ships going to and from China had to pass through the narrow waters.

After Singapore was founded, the British gradually gained control of other Malay states between Singapore and Penang. Between 1874 and 1895 most of the states agreed to allow Great Britain to act as a protector and to have charge of their foreign affairs. In 1885, the sultan of Johore, the southernmost and one of the largest Malay states, made a treaty giving the British many rights. In 1909 several small states in the north were transferred from the control of Siam to that of Britain.

For many years the states of the Malay Peninsula and Singapore were ruled by the British and were called the Straits Settlements. After World War II independence came in several steps. In 1957 the Federation of Malaya was declared an independent member of the British Commonwealth. Singapore also became independent and, in 1963, joined the new Federation of Malaysia. This new Federation of Malaysia consisted of the old Federation of Malaya, Singapore, and two British colonies on the island of Borneo. In

1965 Singapore suddenly decided to leave the federation. We shall read about the reasons for this when we learn more about Singapore.

As we may suppose, there are numerous languages spoken in Malaysia. The Chinese use their own language; the different tribes have different languages. The British taught English in the many schools which they established. Almost all educated people speak English; many have been educated in England. However, the official language of Malaysia is Malay. This language is spoken by Malays in Malaya and in the Indonesian islands.

It is interesting to note that until modern times there was no written Malay language. When a system of writing was developed, the letters of our alphabet were selected. Words are spelled phonetically, or as the words sound. The word for taxi in written Malay is *teksi*. The word for police is *polis*.

The climate of all parts of Malaysia is hot and wet. The equator lies about 80 miles south of the tip of the Malay Peninsula and crosses the middle of Borneo. About 75 percent of Malaysia is jungle. Rainfall averages about 100 inches in most places; on Mount Kinabulu on Borneo, rainfall is more than 400 inches a year! This mountain is 13,455 feet high and is located in Sabah (formerly North Borneo). It is the highest mountain in Southern Asia. The Malay Peninsula is also mountainous, but the mountain ranges are only from 3,000 to 6,000 feet high.

The mountains, jungles, and swamps are filled with animal and bird life. There are many beautiful tropical birds. Among the animals, there are tigers and leopards, rhinoceroses and wild elephants, and many varieties of monkeys of different sizes. In Borneo there is a flying frog able to glide through the air, because of its webbed toes. There are beautiful jungle flowers, including many varieties of orchids. And in Malaya and Borneo there are pitcher plants. These are insect-eating plants with a lid that snaps shut when insects crawl inside the "pitcher." In Malaya, people call one variety the monkey cup. When the lid of the plant is open, the the receptacle catches water, which the wise monkeys drink.

We could write a whole book about the birds, animals, fish, and snakes of the jungles. But now let's read more about the three major parts of the Federation of Malaysia. Malaya is by far the largest, most heavily populated, and most prosperous.

Malaya

As you can see from the map of Southeast Asia, Malaya is a long, narrow country, shaped somewhat like a banana with a stem attached. The southern boundary is the narrow Strait of Johore which separates the Malay Peninsula from the island of Singapore. The country is bounded on the north by narrow pieces of Thailand and Burma which extend down both sides of the narrow peninsula. With an area of 50,690 square miles, Malaya is about the size of the state of Alabama. The population is almost 8,000,000.

About half the population is Malay; almost 40 percent is Chinese; most of the remainder are Tamils from South India. There still are primitive aborigines living deep in the jungles and in the mountains. They are a dying people, however, and each year fewer remain.

We have already seen how Malaya was divided into many states, ruled by sultans. We have also read that the sultans fought one another and were invaded by the seagoing Bugis from the south and by Siam from the north. As the years passed, some of the states were gobbled up. Malaya is now made up of eleven states. These are the old British settlements of Penang and Malacca and the states of Perak, Selangor, Negri Sembilan, Pahang, Johore, Kedah, Perlis, Kelantan, and Trengganu. Nine of the states still have hereditary sultans. The sultans are very wealthy; they sometimes have several palaces, but they have little power. People have regular elections, both for state and national offices. We shall learn more about the government of Malaysia later.

If you were to fly over Malaya, you would see the jungle-covered mountains and hills. In the river valleys there would be rice fields. And you would see two things, both unusual and both having much to do with Malaysia's prosperity. First, you would notice fields and whole hillsides with trees planted in row after row. Next, you would see great raw areas without trees or plants and looking as if bulldozers had been used to scrape and excavate.

The rows of trees are rubber plantations; the bare excavated areas are tin mines. Rubber and tin are the two most important resources and products. Let's first read the interesting story of rubber and how the rubber trees came to Malaya.

The rubber tree is native to the Amazon Valley of South America. For years, raw natural rubber, called latex, came only from Brazil. Many years ago an Englishman smuggled a few rubber seeds out of Brazil. The seeds were planted in the Royal Botanical Gardens in Kew, England, in 1877. The seeds sprouted. The trees were well cared for, and after twenty years there were enough seedlings to plant 360 acres in Malaya.

By 1905 there were about 50,000 acres of land in Malaya planted to rubber trees. It was possible to produce about 200 tons of rubber that year. But much of the world's rubber still came from Brazil. We could say that the people of Brazil killed the goose that laid the golden egg because they forced the price of rubber up and up. Businessmen in Europe and America began to establish rubber plantations in other countries. There was plenty of land available in Malaya and in other parts of Southeast Asia. By 1914 it was possible to deliver Malayan rubber in New York at a cheaper price than South American rubber.

The automobile, more than anything else, made rubber a necessity. The more automobiles that were built, the more rubber was needed, and by 1920 Malaya was producing about 60 percent of the world's supply of natural rubber. Plantations were established in other parts of Southeast Asia, and by 1956, 90 percent of the world's supply of rubber came from Southeast Asia.

During World War II the Japanese controlled the Malay Peninsula, and Allied scientists invented ways of making a synthetic rubber. This is rubber that is made from chemicals rather than from the sap of the rubber trees. Synthetic rubber now accounts for half the world's needs. Of course, this has lowered the price of latex, but natural rubber is still a very important product.

Let's pretend we are visiting a rubber plantation, or estate, as it is called. As we have said, the trees are planted in rows, and most estates are large, covering hundreds or even thousands of acres. When the trees are five or more years old, it is possible to tap them. A circular slanting cut is made in the bark and a little cup fastened near the bottom of the cut. The sap, or latex, runs in the early morning. Each morning the estates are filled with colorfully dressed women who collect the latex. Almost all the women workers are Tamil Indians. The collection is usually finished by eight or nine o'clock. The latex is then taken to a central point to begin a process of drying and curing, after which it is pressed into big sheets for shipment to factories for further processing before being shipped abroad.

Centuries ago, tin was discovered in the Malayan states of Perak, Selangor, and Negri Sembilan. But it was not until about 1850 that tin was mined in large quantities. In that year one of the sultans persuaded thousands of Chinese to

A Malayan rubber tapper.
MALAYSIA DEPT. TOURISM

come to work in the tin mines of Perak. The Chinese were hard workers, and soon thousands of pounds of tin were being exported. As the Chinese saved their money, they began to open shops, banks, and even big stores. They also began to send back to China for their wives and children.

We could say that tin and Chinese in Malaya go together because it was the need for workers in the tin mines which brought Chinese to Malaya in large numbers.

When tin is mined, it is not necessary to go far under the ground. The tin lies very near the surface, and so many parts of Malaya are covered with bare torn-up areas, where big shovels and other mechanical devices have taken the rich soil and extracted tin from it.

In some areas, spices are still important. I have often visited the island of Penang, on the western, or Indian Ocean, side of the Malay Peninsula. Here it is possible to visit plantations where the trees from which we get cloves, nutmeg, and cinnamon are grown.

As we may suppose, there are many varieties of fruit in Malaya. Pineapples have become an important crop, valued at more than $10,000,000 annually. There are two other interesting fruits, not grown for export, but popular in Malaysia and other parts of Southeast Asia. The jackfruit and the duarian look somewhat alike. Somewhat spiny, these fruits grow to the size of a football. The duarian is rather unusual because it smells like rotten eggs. Yet the fruit is quite tasty.

Finally, we should mention coconut palms and rice. The dried meat of the coconut, called copra, is rich in oil used in making soap, cooking oil, and margarine. And rice is the most important food of all Malaysians, regardless of race. Rice is grown wherever there is flat and easily irrigated land.

Even though there are many mountains and hills, as well as swamps, Malaya has an excellent highway system. The British built good roads and railroads as well. It is possible to reach almost all major cities by road and railroad. And of course, there are modern airfields and airlines that connect all the big cities.

Kuala Lumpur, with almost 500,000 persons, is Malaya's largest city and the capital of the Malaysian Federation. K.L., as it is called, is a modern city. It is largely a new city, since it is the capital of a new nation. The government buildings, the national university, and other buildings are modern and very beautiful. The city of George Town on the island of Penang is the second largest city and Malaysia's most important port. With a population of more than 200,000, George Town is reached from the mainland by ferry or by air.

Malaya is prosperous and well developed. Now we will visit the parts of Malaysia that are quite different. Borneo is the world's largest island, next to Greenland and New

Guinea. It contains some of the world's wildest and least known mountains and jungles.

Sarawak and Sabah

During the years when the British and Dutch were fighting over Southeast Asia, Borneo was divided. The northern one-fourth was taken by the British; the rest, by the Dutch. The Dutch part is now called Kalimantan and is a part of the Republic of Indonesia.

Let's look at the map of Southeast Asia. You will see that the whole northern coast of Borneo is not a part of Indonesia. Both Sarawak and Sabah are parts of the Malaysian Federation. A small area, called Brunei, decided not to join the federation and is a British protectorate.

With an area of 48,250 square miles and a population of more than 800,000, Sarawak has a very strange history. At one time this area as large as many of our states belonged to one man. His name was James Brooke. He and his son are the only Europeans who ever became rajas, ruling a whole country.

James Brooke was the son of a British civil servant in India. In 1830 he sailed on a trip to China. When his ship passed through the islands south and east of Singapore, he was impressed with their beauty, but he also noticed that the seas around Borneo were filled with pirates and that different sultans were always fighting one another.

After his father died, Brooke became wealthy. He bought a 140-ton yacht, which he named the *Royalist*. With a picked crew, Brooke sailed for Borneo, hoping to explore the big island. When he arrived, he found the district of Sarawak in revolt against the sultan of Brunei. In addition, there was a rebellion among the fierce headhunting aborigines known as Dyaks. Finally, the whole coast of Borneo was being raided by pirate gangs. There were Dyak pirates and fierce pirates from the Philippines, called Lanuns.

The sultan of Sarawak offered to make Brooke governor of the district if he would help fight the pirates and the rebels. James Brooke accepted. The small crew of the *Royalist* was well trained. Brooke quickly trained several score Malay seamen so that he had a small navy. With his own men and sometimes with the help of the British navy, Brooke fought the pirates all along the coast of Borneo. He defeated the Dyaks and the Lanuns, attacking and burning the pirate villages.

In 1846, Sultan Omar of Brunei ceded Sarawak to James Brooke. He became sole owner and ruler of the whole district.

It was necessary for Brooke to fight the pirates for several years. But by 1849 he had completely defeated them. Since the pirates often attacked shipping in the Strait of Malacca and around Singapore, Brooke's victory was very important. For the first time in history it was possible for traders to pass through these waters in safety.

James Brooke was knighted and, as Sir James the White Raja, ruled the people of Sarawak with justice until his son, Charles, became raja. It was during the reign of Charles Brooke that an interesting event occurred.

Charles Brooke decided that if his little kingdom was to

become prosperous, he needed other people besides Malays and Dyaks. There were a few Chinese in Borneo, and in 1899 Raja Brooke asked one of the leading Chinese to go back to China and secure colonists.

This Chinese, named Uong Nai-siong, happened to be a Christian. He returned to his native village near the South China coast. Since he was a Christian, he invited friends and relatives who were also Christians to join him in Sarawak. Two great seagoing junks were filled with colonists and set sail from the port of Foochow.

The seas were rough, but after six days two junks arrived in Hong Kong. Most of the colonists were seasick and homesick and ready to go back home. It just happened that an American missionary was in Hong Kong, on his way from India to the United States. He heard about the Christian Chinese. There was only one man aboard the two ships who could speak English. The American missionary found this one man, heard the story, and learned that the Chinese were about to give up. Saving the day, he told them that if they would sail on to Singapore and Borneo, he would give up his trip to America and go with them, instead.

So it was that about 1,000 Christian Chinese arrived in Sarawak in 1901. Thousands more have followed, until now there are more than 250,000 Chinese, making up nearly 30 percent of the population. About 40 percent of these Chinese are Christians.

The Brooke family found that in modern times it is difficult for one family to rule a whole country. In 1946 the fam-

Many of the tribespeople of Borneo are Dyaks. This is a Dyak chief.

ily gave Sarawak to Great Britain, and it became a British crown colony. In 1963 it became a state in the Federation of Malaysia. Kuching, a city of 50,000 persons, is the capital.

As in Malaya, there are different races in Sarawak. There are many Malays and several hundred thousand tribespeople. There are many different tribes. The best known are the Dyaks (pronounced DIE-aks).

Until a few years ago many of the Dyaks were fierce people who were headhunters. Away from the cities, they are still primitive and wear almost no clothes. Most Dyaks live in longhouses. A longhouse is just what it says — a very long house, set on stilts and divided into rooms for the many families who live there. There is a picture of a very long longhouse on the next page. The Dyaks also have longboats.

47

The Dyaks live in "Long Houses". LOUIS DENNIS

These are very narrow boats, each made by hollowing out one huge jungle tree. Now, as the Dyaks are becoming civilized, they attach an outboard motor to their longboats and are able to move up and down the rivers at great speed.

Sabah lies along the coast of Borneo, north and east of Sarawak. It is much smaller than Sarawak, both in area and population. The capital is Jesselton, with a population of 25,000. For many years known as the British crown colony of North Borneo, Sabah became a part of the federation in 1963.

We have mentioned Mount Kinabulu, the highest peak in Southeast Asia. It is located in the northern part of Sabah. The tribe called the Dusuns worships the mountain, which it believes is the gate to heaven.

Sabah and Sarawak produce some rubber, much pepper, sego (which is flour made from the inside of the sego palm tree), and some forest products from the tropical jungles.

It is interesting to know that black pepper comes from a vine that is trained to grow around a stake about ten feet high. If you fly over Sarawak, it is easy to spot the pepper fields scattered through the jungle, for each pepper vine is set an exact distance from its neighbor. From the air the pepper vines make a beautiful and clear pattern.

There is one other product of Sarawak that is very interesting. Perhaps you have heard of a rare dish called bird's-nest soup. It is considered a great delicacy by the Chinese. In many places in Sarawak there are caves where tiny birds, like our chimney swifts, build their nests. The nests are made of saliva from the birds' mouths. It is sticky and yellow but becomes hard and dry in the air. The nests look like small saucers stuck to the sides of the caves. The people who live near the caves build long bamboo ladders so that they can climb along the sides and collect the nests. Then they sell the nests to Chinese for bird's-nest soup.

Even though it decided not to belong to the Malaysian Federation, this is a good place to mention the British protectorate of Brunei. This sultanate lies on the coast of Borneo between Sarawak and Sabah. The area is 2,226 square miles, and the population is less than 100,000. The people of Brunei decided not to join the federation in 1963. Their ruler is a sultan who rules with the advice and protection of Great Britain. Brunei is chiefly important because of its oil deposits. The Seria oil fields produce about 5,000,000 tons of oil each year. This makes Brunei second to Canada in oil production among British Commonwealth nations.

The Government of Malaysia

We have read that Malaysia was formed in 1963. The government is a democracy somewhat like that of Great Britain. The leader of a party winning an election becomes the chief of state, called the prime minister. The prime minister has much the same power as does our President. We would call the government a constitutional monarchy but with one unusual difference from other nations whose chief of state is a king or queen. In Malaysia the king is elected for a four-year term. The nine hereditary sultans elect one of their number to serve as the king, who has no political power.

Each of the thirteen states elects a state Assembly and a representative to the national Parliament, which meets at Kuala Lumpur. Members of the national Senate are elected to six-year terms; members of the House of Representatives, to five-year terms. Each state has its own flag, which flies by the side of the national flag of Malaysia.

We have read that Malay is the national language. Malay and English are the official languages. This means that government business can be transacted in either language.

Malaysia has faced difficult problems. For almost ten years after World War II there was a war with the Communists in the jungles of Malaya. This war was much like the fighting against the Vietcong in Vietnam. British and Malayan soldiers finally won this bitter and expensive war in 1958.

Another problem has been relations between the Malays and the Chinese, who have become the most successful businessmen. In order to protect the Malays, the Malay-controlled national government has passed laws that discriminate against the Chinese. For instance, three-fourths of all government jobs must go to Malays.

It was this discrimination against the Chinese that led to the withdrawal of Singapore from the federation in 1965. We shall read more about this in the next section. Another problem in the past few years has been the threats from big neighbor Indonesia. This country is ten times as big as Malaysia and has been threatening to attack and conquer its small neighbor. However, in 1966 Indonesia had a change in government, and there are better relations between the two countries.

It was unfortunate for both Singapore and Malaysia when the former decided to withdraw from the federation. Now we shall read about Singapore, the island nation that lies less than a mile off the southern tip of the Malay Peninsula. Even though Malaysia and Singapore are separate nations, both belong to the British Commonwealth, and they still use the same money and the same postage stamps.

SINGAPORE

Like Hong Kong, Singapore is an island. But it is connected to the mainland by a causeway, or bridge. The map shows us that Singapore lies just south of the southern tip of the Malay Peninsula. It is less than a mile across the causeway to the Malayan state of Johore.

Singapore is only 80 miles north of the equator. The

climate is hot, and the rainfall heavy. The area is 217 square miles, almost eight times the area of Hong Kong Island. The population is 1,900,000 and growing very fast. Almost 80 percent of the population is Chinese. Malays are the second largest group, and there are numerous Indians, Pakistanis, and Europeans.

Singapore was founded by the British as a trading port and to control the narrow Strait of Malacca. We have read that the strait connects the Indian Ocean with the part of the Pacific Ocean known as the South China Sea.

If you were to visit Singapore, you would see many places named for an Englishman, Sir Stamford Raffles. There is a Raffles Place, a Raffles Hotel, and statues of Raffles. Stamford Raffles was an official of the British East India Company. In 1810 he was appointed agent to the Malay states.

Raffles decided that Great Britain must have a trading post and naval base closer to the tip of Malaya than Penang. In 1819 he selected the island of Singa Pura, which means the Lion City in the Sanskrit language. There were no lions, and we are not certain how this name came about. Also, there was no city at that time. The population consisted of about 5,000 Malay fishermen.

Within a year the population had doubled. Raffles considered the Malays a lazy people. So he sent to China for settlers. Soon thousands of Chinese began coming to Singapore, and much credit is due them for making Singapore a great city. However, it was Raffles who was in every way the father of Singapore. He drafted laws to prevent slave trade, organized a police system, laid out the port, and even planned the streets of the city.

Stamford Raffles would certainly be surprised if he could visit Singapore today. Notice the pictures on the adjacent pages. You can see that Singapore is a modern city with fine buildings and wide streets. Its port is the sixth largest and busiest in the world.

We have read that the majority of the population is Chinese. There are nearly 1,500,000 Chinese in Singapore. So Singapore, which is more than 1,500 miles from China, is one of the largest Chinese cities in the world. In addition, there are about 200,000 Malays and many Indians and Pakistanis. Singapore is an international city, inhabited by people of different nationalities.

In the city there are newspapers published in four different languages: English, Chinese, Tamil, and Malay. There are English-language schools, Chinese-language schools, and Malay-language schools. But since Great Britain controlled Singapore for many years, nearly all educated people speak English.

The history of Singapore is, of course, like that of Malaya. We have already read about the pirates and the wars between different sultans and between the European powers for control of the area. From 1819 until 1856 Singapore was ruled by the British East India Company. Then, for a few years, it was a part of India. From 1886 to 1942 it was one of the British-controlled Straits Settlements.

On February 15, 1942, the Japanese army conquered the

city, and it was under Japanese rule until the end of World War II. The story of Singapore's capture is interesting. We have read that it was a British naval base. The British did not believe that any army could march through the jungles of Malaya. Therefore, all the big guns were pointed out to sea. The British thought that an attack, if it came, would be from the sea. But the Japanese landed on the coast of the Malay Peninsula, marched through the jungles, and attacked from the rear, or land, side. There was no time to turn all the big guns around. The city fell in a few weeks' time.

Singapore became a British crown colony in 1946 and an independent and self-governing part of the British family of nations in 1959. When the Federation of Malaysia was established in 1963, it was joined by Singapore. A majority of the citizens of Malaysia are Malays, and we have already learned that most of the people in Singapore are Chinese. This led to Singapore's withdrawal from Malaysia in the summer of 1965. Its people, largely Chinese, were afraid that they would become too much under the control of Malays.

Singapore, therefore, is now an independent country. We should probably call it an independent city-state. It is a member of the British Commonwealth of Nations, and Great Britain has promised to protect it from invaders. The government of Singapore is like that of Great Britain. There are elections, and the head of the party which wins an election becomes the prime minister. There is an Assembly which makes laws and operates as our Congress does. Singapore, of course, has its own flag, but since it withdrew from Malaysia, it has used the same currency and the same stamps that áre used by that country. This may be changed, or it is possible that the leaders and people of Singapore will change their minds and once again join Malaysia.

Singapore is important for several reasons. Even though it is independent, the British have an important naval base in the city, and it is headquarters for all British Commonwealth forces in the Far East. Its harbor is one of the largest and best in the world. Of course, now that people travel as much by plane as by ship, Singapore is not as important as it once was. In other words, a city can no longer control an area as Singapore once controlled the Strait of Malacca.

Part of Singapore's importance was that most of the raw rubber from Malaya was processed and shipped throughout the world from its great harbor. Also, the tin from Malaya was largely shipped from Singapore. Now that Singapore no longer belongs to the federation, Malaysia is trying to develop its own ports.

In Singapore there is a hill called Mount Faber. If you stand on the top of Mount Faber and look south, you can see some of the islands belonging to Indonesia. We have read that Indonesia has caused trouble for Malaysia. This policy was started while Singapore was a part of Malaysia. The Indonesians often landed guerrilla fighters on Singapore Island. Indonesia stopped all trade between itself and Singapore and Malaysia. Hundreds of small trading ships were tied up in Singapore's harbor because of this policy. This "country" is too small to have an army. Were it not for the fact that both Singapore and Malaysia belong to the British Commonwealth and are under British protection, Indonesia would probably have invaded both. Thousands of British and Australian soldiers in Singapore and Malaysia kept the Indonesians out.

We have read that the British built good roads and railroads in Malaya. They also provided good schools and health services in their Malayan colonies. As a result, Singapore, Kuala Lumpur, George Town, and the other cities of Malaya are clean and attractive. It is safe to drink water from the tap in these cities. This is unusual in Asia, where the water supply of most big cities is unfit for drinking unless it is first boiled to kill the germs.

The Republic of Indonesia

Now let's visit the Republic of Indonesia, a nation of 3,000 islands that begin within sight of Singapore.

In area and population, Indonesia is the largest nation in Southeast Asia. The area is 735,000 square miles, or about one-fifth the size of the United States, but the population of more than 105,000,000 persons is more than half that of our country. In population, Indonesia is the fifth largest nation in the world.

The map shows us that the islands of Indonesia begin close to Singapore and extend for a distance of 3,300 miles from east to west, all the way to the southern islands of the

Philippines. The equator runs through the nations, so we may expect that the weather is tropical — hot and very wet. During the monsoon season, from November to February, rainfall is very heavy. In some parts of Indonesia, 240 inches of rain fall each year.

The Indonesian islands are volcanic. There are more than 700 volcanoes, many of them still active. In 1883 an island suddenly appeared in the ocean in a huge eruption. Called Krakatau, this island was born in an eruption that created a tidal wave that reached New York City in fourteen and one-half hours!

In Indonesia there are vast jungles, many highly cultivated areas, high mountains, heavily populated islands, and numerous small islands populated only with wild animals and snakes. There are tigers, orangutans, and many other wild animals and birds in the Indonesian jungles. On one island, named Komodo, there are lizards that are twelve feet long. When the European explorers discovered these huge lizards, they thought that they were seeing real dragons.

Archaeologists have found the fossil remains of early man on the Indonesian island of Java. Perhaps man got his start in this part of the world. In prehistoric times there were also migrations of people from the mainland of Asia. More than 2,000 years ago visitors and settlers began to come to the islands from the west. These sailors and traders were from India. They brought the Hindu and Buddhist religions to Indonesia. The Indians also brought their written language, called Sanskrit, so that we have some records of the different empires that flourished for almost 2,000 years.

We do not have space to tell about the ancient nations, some powerful and some small. For several centuries there was a powerful Hindu kingdom called the Majapahit. By the seventh and eighth centuries powerful Buddhist kingdoms had arisen in Indonesia. One line of kings was called the Sailendras. They were so powerful at one time that their kingdom included parts of Malaya and Thailand. The Sailendras built a great city of Buddhist temples at Borobudur in Java. A Sailendra king began to build the greatest of these temples in A.D. 772.

In 1478 new invaders began to conquer most of the islands of Indonesia. These people were Moslems, the religion we have already read about and the one to which most Malayans belong. Today more than 80 percent of the population is Moslem. There are some Christians and very few Buddhists, and the people of the small island of Bali are still Hindus.

The Moslem religion was founded by Mohammed, who lived in Arabia in the sixth and seventh centuries. Moslems, or Mohammedans, believe in one God. Their Bible is called the Koran. Moslem places of worship are called mosques (pronounced mosks).

In 1596 the Dutch established trading posts and soon controlled most of the islands. The Dutch and other Europeans were looking for spices and other treasures. When Columbus sailed across the Atlantic in 1492, he was looking for a short cut to the Spice Islands.

The Dutch established a trading company called the Dutch East India Company and named their colony the Dutch, or Netherlands, East Indies. They made their headquarters in the city of Jakarta (also spelled Djakarta), which they called Batavia. The Dutch ruled from this city for more than 300 years.

Before we learn more of the history and government of Indonesia, let's read about the most important of the 3,000 islands. Almost three-fourths of the island of Borneo belongs to Indonesia and is called Kalimantan. Except for areas along the coast and one area rich in oil, Kalimantan is wild, jungle country.

Next to Kalimantan in size is the island of Sumatra, which forms the southern side of the Strait of Malacca. Much of this island is wild and unexplored with many animals, including tigers and orangutans. However, some of the richest oil fields in the world are located along the northeast coast of Sumatra.

Java is the third largest of the islands. It is one of the most densely populated areas in the world. Almost three-fourths of Indonesia's population lives on this island.

We have mentioned the small island of Bali, unusual because its people are still Hindus. This island is well known to many people because of its beauty, its many Hindu temples, and the music and dancing of its people.

Rice fields on island of Java.   AID

Among other important islands are Sulawesi (formerly the Celebes) and a group of islands called the Moluccas, the proper name for the Spice Islands so sought by European sea captains and traders. Indonesia also controls the western end of the big island of New Guinea.

In Indonesia, as in Malaysia, there are numerous racial groups. These include many primitive tribespeople and several million Chinese. A majority of the people are Malays. Malay is the official and national language. Written Malay is almost exactly like the written Malay used in Malaysia.

The Dutch were efficient but rather cruel rulers. They were interested in making money, not in helping Indonesians. They developed large spice plantations. Rubber was introduced from Malaya and became a very important resource. Coffee and cacao (from which we get cocoa) became important crops. The great oil deposits of Sumatra and Borneo were developed. Rice is the main food of the people, and under some governors, the people were forced to grow spices instead of rice. This caused widespread starvation.

In Malaya the British built roads and established many schools and hospitals. There was opportunity for many people to become educated. But the Dutch did not want educated Indonesians. When Indonesia did become independent, there were almost no Indonesian doctors, engineers, or other trained people.

Independence came after a long and cruel Japanese occupation during World War II. The Dutch were defeated and driven out by the Japanese. When the war ended, the Dutch came back. But the cruel Japanese occupation had driven many young Indonesians into the mountains and jungles, where they became guerrilla fighters. The people who had suffered so much under Japanese rule were determined to drive out the Dutch.

For several years there was bitter fighting between the island people and the Dutch. The revolution against the Dutch finally ended in 1949. The Dutch agreed to give up the islands, and for the first time in many centuries the people were free and independent.

Unfortunately, the government of the Republic of Indonesia has been inefficient and corrupt. In part, we could blame this on the Dutch. We have read that few Indonesians became educated during the years of Dutch rule. There were too few Indonesians capable of government leadership.

The Indonesians were bitterly anti-Dutch and soon became just as opposed to our country. Even though the United States gave millions of dollars in economic aid, Indonesian leaders distrusted us because we had been allied with the Dutch. The government more and more turned to Russia and Communist China for help.

By 1966 Indonesia had the largest Communist party in the world, next to those in Russia and China. The government had become more and more pro-Communist. American Peace Corps workers were asked to leave the country. The U.S. aid program was closed down. American- and British-owned buildings were often attacked and sometimes burned. All American and British property, including rich oil fields, was taken over by the Indonesian government. Indonesia even resigned from the United Nations.

All this changed suddenly when the Communists tried to take complete control in 1966. Army generals and others opposed to Communism were murdered. However, other generals and many Moslem leaders who were opposed to Communism fought back and defeated the Communists. All through 1966 there was bloodshed, with tens of thousands of Communists, or people suspected of being Communists, murdered or imprisoned.

As a result, Indonesia is no longer allied with the Communist world. The Communist party has been outlawed.

The government is once again being friendly to the Western nations and is rejoining the United Nations. Unfortunately, the years of pro-Communist government have almost wrecked the country. Inflation is so bad that when people go to market, they must carry a suitcase full of money. In times of inflation everything costs so much; and because wages and salaries do not go up, many people do not have enough money to buy food.

Highways and railroads have not been kept in repair. Factories are shut down. People are starving because farmers have not been able to grow enough food. We could say that Indonesia is a bankrupt country. Its people have never had

A roadside market ·   ICA

real democracy. Millions of dollars have been wasted on worthless projects or on the campaign to conquer Malaysia and Singapore.

We hope that Indonesia's new and anti-Communist government will be able to repair the damage of years of misrule. Indonesia is rich in natural resources. It need not be a poor and bankrupt nation. With help from the United States and other Western nations, we hope that this beautiful country will soon be on its feet.

The Buddhist Nations of Southeast Asia

Gautama, who became known as Buddha (which means Enlightened One), was born in India in 563 B.C. The religion he founded is followed by 175,000,000 persons. Buddha believed that evil could be overcome by contemplation, which means by study and thought, rather than by action. Buddhists believe that the less we want and the more we use self-control and right thinking, the happier our lives will be. The followers of Buddha have built countless beautiful temples in the Far East. In each temple there are usually several large images of Buddha, as well as of sages and gods. Buddhists worship the images.

There are some Buddhists in every country in Southeast Asia, but there are three nations in which Buddhism is the state religion. This means that it is the official religion of the people.

Let's look at the map of Southeast Asia again. The Buddhist countries begin at the northern boundary of Malaya. They are Thailand, Cambodia, and Laos. So you can see that this part of Asia is an important Buddhist center. One-third of all the Buddhists in the world live here.

THAILAND, OR SIAM

Thailand, for many years called Siam, is the largest of the three Buddhist nations we will visit. By looking at the map, you see that it is located in the middle of the big part of the Southeast Asian peninsula. A long narrow sliver of Thailand extends down the Malay Peninsula toward Singapore. On the west, Thailand is bounded by Burma; on the south, by the Gulf of Siam; on the east and north, by Cambodia and Laos.

The area of Thailand is just over 200,000 square miles, somewhat smaller than Texas. The population is 30,000,000. We can understand that Thailand is a Buddhist country from these figures: in 1966 there were 162,000 Buddhist monks and 19,150 temples and monasteries!

We call the people of Thailand, Thais (pronounced tiez), and they are related to the Chinese. It is possible that they came to Thailand from some place in Central Asia. There are also numerous tribes, the aborigines of Thailand, who live in the mountains. And there are about 4,000,000 Chinese.

There are mountain ranges in the north and northwest. The highest peak is 8,452 feet. The land becomes lower to the south and is flat near the Gulf of Siam. The largest river is called the Chao Phraya, and Bangkok, the capital, is located on this river 30 miles from the ocean.

The climate is hot and humid. The monsoon season begins in late May and lasts until September. During this period the rain comes every day.

Thai history goes back for hundreds of years. There were periods when the Thais were very powerful, ruling much of Southeast Asia. Thailand became a crossroads between India and China, and its people borrowed ideas from both countries. There is a written language that is based on Sanskrit, the language of ancient India. The spoken language is somewhat like Chinese, with five tones. By this we mean that each spoken word can have five different meanings, depending on the inflection, or tone of one's voice.

Temples of ancient capital of Ayut'ia.   TOT

The first great Thai kingdom was called Sukhot'ai, and it began in 1238. Under the rule of King Rama the Brave from 1283 to 1317, the Thais became the most civilized nation in Southeast Asia. During this period the written language was developed.

The kingdom of Ayut'ia became even more powerful. During this dynasty the Thais conquered the Khmers of Cambodia and destroyed their great capital city of Angkor. We will read about Angkor in the next section. The last powerful dynasty, or line of rulers, is known as the Bangkok Dynasty. It began after the death of the last Ayut'ian king in 1767. The present king of Thailand is the ninth ruler in this dynasty.

Thailand is more prosperous than its neighbors, and it was never conquered by the Europeans for several reasons. The kings of ancient Thailand decreed that all farmers should own their own land. In other Asian countries most farmland was owned by rich landlords. The farmer was merely a tenant.

Some of the early kings were also good politicians. We might say they knew how to play one side against another. The European nations were very anxious to trade with Thailand. In 1602 the Dutch opened a trading post in the city of Patani. In 1612 King James I of England sent a special emissary to Thailand. But whenever it looked as if the Dutch were getting too strong, the Thai kings would make friends with the English or French. For 200 years the Thais managed to play the French, Dutch, and English against one another. Even during World War II they played both sides. Seeing that Japan was about to conquer all Southeast Asia, Thailand declared war on the United States and Britain. But although they were at war with us, the Thai people were very friendly. They hid many American secret agents in Bangkok, right under the noses of the Japanese!

Another reason Thailand remained free is that under the kings of the Bangkok Dynasty, Thailand became interested in Western ways. King Rama IV, or Mongkut, as he was called, learned to speak English from American missionaries. He made friends with Englishmen and Americans. In 1855 he signed a treaty of friendship with Great Britain, and in 1856 similar treaties were made with America and France.

King Mongkut decided that his son must learn English, too. In 1862 he employed an Englishwoman to teach all the royal children. Her name was Mrs. Anna Leonowens. A famous book called *Anna and the King of Siam* was written about this woman. Later the book was made into a play. And then the play was made into a motion picture, called *The King and I*.

King Mongkut and his son Rama V, or Chulalongkorn, did much to make Thailand more modern than its neighbors. Rama V traveled to Europe. He was the first Thai king who drove about the city in public and actually talked to his subjects. He tried to abolish slavery. When Rama V came to the throne, Bangkok had no streets. People traveled over a vast system of canals, called klongs. There are still some klongs; but under Rama V, streets were built, and the construction of the first railroad was begun.

In 1932 Thailand became a constitutional monarchy. This means that the power of the king is limited, just as in England. There are elections, and the real ruler is the prime minister, who has much the same authority as our President.

In 1939 the government decided not to use the old name of Siam anymore. The official name of the country became Muang Thai, which means Land of the Free. However, many Thais still like the old name. There is talk that the name may be changed back to Siam. Thailand's flag is red,

A man delivering coconuts in Bangkok.   AID

white, and blue, like our flag. There are five horizontal stripes — red, white, blue, white, red.

The Thais certainly have more freedom than their neighbors and are more prosperous. In other countries of Asia two or sometimes three crops of rice are grown each year. In Thailand there is only one rice crop. The harvest is so abundant that Thailand is the world's greatest exporter of rice. Next to rice in importance are tin (Thailand is the world's third producer of tin ore); teak from the tropical forests; some rubber; coconuts; and fruits.

In Thailand there is compulsory and free education. This means that all boys and girls must go to school, and there is no cost. Many schools are operated by the government, but

This is the floating market in Bangkok.   AID

many others are operated by Buddhists. In fact, almost every big Buddhist temple operates a school. Because of these policies, almost everyone in Thailand can read and write.

We have mentioned that Bangkok has many canals, or klongs. There are still hundreds of canals in the broad flat plains of south Thailand. Many boys and girls go to school by boat. There are even water taxis to take people to work. And farmers still take their crops to a big floating market near Bangkok each morning. Housewives come in their boats to buy the day's food.

Bangkok, the capital, has a population of almost 3,000,000. There are still numerous klongs, but there also are many wide paved streets. It is a city of beautiful temples. Among

Thailand is a country of many temples.

TOT

these are the Temple of the Emerald Buddha, where the king often worships; the Temple of the Dawn; the Temple of the Reclining Buddha; and the beautiful Marble Temple. In one temple there is a solid-gold image of Buddha worth $36,000,000.

We have learned that there are about 4,000,000 Chinese in Thailand. Each city has its large Chinatown. There are many Chinese stores, schools, and newspapers. As in much of Southeast Asia, the Chinese are hardworking business-men, who control much of the business.

There are many automobiles in Bangkok and Chiengmai, the only other large city. But many people still travel in a mechanized pedicab called a trishaw, which means a three-wheeler. A motorcycle is attached to a small covered cab.

The Wat Arun, or Temple of the Dawn, in Bangkok.

Elephants are work animals in Southeast Asia.

American tourists like to visit Thailand. It is possible to visit jungle areas and watch elephants working in the teak forests. Each year there is an elephant roundup, when young wild elephants are captured so they may be trained as work animals.

But Thailand also has numerous problems. The people of the dry northeast are poor. There are numerous diseases and as yet too few doctors and hospitals. Many farmers still use primitive farming methods. Our government has been helping Thailand for several years. American experts teach Thais about modern agriculture and public health, and how to build and operate factories. There are many Peace Corps workers who teach village people and farmers modern ways of doing things.

Through American aid, several fine highways have been built. Several big dams for making electric power and for irrigation have also been built with American aid. Some of Bangkok's big wide streets where there used to be canals have been built with American aid.

Thailand and the United States are allies. Both countries belong to SEATO, the Southeast Asia Treaty Organization. SEATO headquarters are in Bangkok. Our country is pledged to help Thailand if it is attacked by another country. Thailand in turn has helped and is helping our country. Many of the American planes that bomb North Vietnam fly from air bases in Thailand.

Thailand's biggest problem may come from Communist China. The Communists have announced they intend to conquer Thailand in one way or another. Communist agents and terrorists are beginning to attack isolated villages. Just as the Vietcong have done, Communists are kidnapping or murdering village leaders and schoolteachers. Actually, Thailand is more important to the Communists than Vietnam. China cannot grow enough food for its huge population. We have read that Thai farmers grow so much rice that millions of tons are sold to other rice-eating nations. The Communists would like to control the rice, as well as other resources of Thailand.

In spite of threats from China, Thailand has remained one of the United States' best friends in Asia. Its people are grateful for American aid. Its government has refused to be frightened by Communist threats. In the next section we will read about Thailand's neighbors who have become almost completely Communist-controlled.

THE KINGDOM OF CAMBODIA

Cambodia lies to the east of Thailand. It has an area of 69,866 square miles, which is almost exactly the size of the state of Missouri. The population is about 6,000,000. The capital is Pnompenh, with a population of 600,000. The capital city is located on the Mekong River, one of the largest rivers in the world.

Like Thailand, Cambodia is a Buddhist country, and its history goes back many centuries. We know about the history of this little country from the Chinese, who invented a way of writing centuries ago and kept records that are very helpful today. Also like Thailand, Cambodia was greatly influenced by India.

There were powerful Hindu kingdoms in Cambodia almost 2,000 years ago. We do not have space to discuss all these kingdoms of the past. We shall read about the most interesting Cambodian kingdom, which came into power in A.D. 802. We could say that Cambodia is mainly important and famous because of this dynasty, known as the Khmers.

The Khmers (pronounced almost as come-HERE or c'm-'ERE) ruled from their capital at Angkor for six centuries. The city of Angkor was founded in 889. For the next 300 years the king and his followers built huge temples and cities over an area of sixty square miles! The temples were built with great blocks of sandstone, which were cut from quarries a long distance away. These great blocks of stone were floated downriver by raft, then moved by elephants and slave labor to the temple and city sites.

Angkor Wat is the most famous and the largest temple. It is one of the most unusual buildings in all the world. The Banteay Srei, or Citadel of Women, is another one of the famous Khmer temples. On this page you can see a picture of the Angkor Wat and some of the other temples.

All the kings in the Khmer Dynasty had Indian names, and the way of writing that was developed came from the Indian Sanskrit. At first these great temples were Hindu, but later they became places of Buddhist worship. And so in these temples we can see Hindu gods, as well as huge Bud-

This is the huge Temple of Angkor Wat.

dhas. Shortly after the end of the twelfth century the people became Buddhist, and they have been Buddhist ever since.

The Khmer kings were great builders but not always good generals. The war with the Thais went on for years until the Thais finally captured Angkor in 1431. They killed thousands of people and took thousands of captives. The Khmer kings moved from place to place, finally settling at Pnompenh, which is still the capital. But the Khmer power was gone, and the people never again had powerful rulers.

The climate of Cambodia is very hot and wet, and trees grow fast. Soon the scores of temples, or wats, as they are called, were covered by the jungle. For more than 500 years the magnificent temples of Angkor were forgotten. In the nineteenth century, however, a French archaeologist discovered the buried city. Angkor Thom, which means the city of Angkor, and Angkor Wat, the main temple, soon became one of the great wonders of Asia. The French cleared away the jungle growth from the main buildings, and to this day thousands of people are able to come and see these magnificent structures built more than 1,000 years ago.

In the first part of this book we learned that the French gained control over a large part of Southeast Asia. When the French were unable to open trading posts in Thailand, they turned their attention to the eastern part of the big Indochinese Peninsula. By either conquest or threats, the French eventually controlled all this area, from the borders of China to the Gulf of Siam.

In the case of Cambodia, the French offered to protect the

weak Cambodian king from the Thais and Vietnamese who were always nibbling at Cambodian territory. Once the French had gained the advantage, they moved fast. In 1884 the king of Cambodia was forced to sign another agreement, placing all real authority in the hands of the French. By 1887 French control was complete. In that year the Indochinese Union, a French colony, was formed.

French Indochina, as it was called, was divided into three parts: Cambodia, Laos, and Vietnam. The kings of these countries were allowed to keep their thrones, but all authority rested with the French, who had their main offices in the modern city of Saigon. In another section of this book we shall learn about the wars which started soon after World War II and eventually resulted in the freedom and independence of this area.

Now let's learn something about modern Cambodia. The map shows us that Cambodia is almost square. In the west, it has a long boundary with Thailand, and in the east, a long boundary with Vietnam. The short northern boundary is with Laos, and in the south, Cambodia is bounded by the Gulf of Siam.

The population of Cambodia is almost 6,000,000. No one can know exactly how many people there are, for Cambodia has many square miles of wild jungle and swamp land. There are even villages built on stilts, completely surrounded by water. If you lived in one of these villages and wanted to visit your neighbors, you would have to use a boat.

The jungles are inhabited by many wild animals. In fact, Cambodia is one of the best big-game hunting places in the world. There are herds of wild elephants, wild bulls, buffaloes, tigers, panthers, and several kinds of deer.

As we have said, the climate of Cambodia is hot. From May to October there is a season of heavy rain. Then, from November through April, there is a dry season. But there always seems to be too much water. Near the old city of Ankor there is a very large lake called the Tonle Sap. And the Mekong, one of the longest rivers in the world, flows through Cambodia and then into South Vietnam.

Pnompenh, the capital city, is located on the Mekong River. It can be reached from the Gulf of Siam by ocean-going ships.

Cambodia is a primitive country, with few highways or railways. About 50 percent of the area is still virgin jungle. The French developed some rubber plantations. But most cultivated land is used for growing rice, which is the main food of Cambodia. The forests produce some timber, and there is some production of spices.

The people of Cambodia have their own language, both spoken and written. The written language is related to Sanskrit. Almost all well-educated people speak French, because France controlled the country for seventy-five years. French is called the second language of Cambodia and is used on postage stamps and on money.

Cambodia became an independent constitutional monarchy after World War II. The king has no power. The constitution provides that the people elect representatives to a National Assembly like our Congress, and the prime minister is the chief executive. Unfortunately, Cambodia has not had honest or real elections and must be called a dictatorship.

For several years our government gave much economic aid to Cambodia. At the same time the Cambodians were accepting help from Communist China and Russia. Slowly the country has become more and more anti-American and more interested in the Communist way of life. In 1963 Cambodia broke off all relations with our country. American help and advice are no longer welcome. The country has allied itself completely with the Communist world.

Being a Buddhist country, Cambodia has many temples and monasteries. We hope that there will be a change and that some time Cambodia will again be friendly to the United States. It is an interesting and beautiful country, the ruins of Angkor are among the wonders of the world, and we should like to be able to visit them.

Although some progress has been made with the aid of the Communists, Cambodia is still very poor and underdeveloped. It has little trade with the rest of the world. Pnompenh, which used to be an attractive city, is now dirty and shabby. The streets in the city and the few highways in the country badly need repairs. The economy of the country is in almost as bad condition as that of Indonesia.

Laos, Land of a Million Elephants

The kingdom of Laos (pronounced almost like louse) is one of the least developed countries in the world. There are no railroads and almost no highways. Until recently there was no newspaper or even a printing press in the whole country. The area of Laos is 91,000 square miles, which is about the size of Kansas. The population is estimated by the government to be 3,000,000, but no one really knows how many people there are. There are many wild mountains which have never even been explored. The population is probably 2,000,000 or less.

Many years ago Laos was known as the Land of a Million Elephants. There are many elephants, even on the main street of the capital city. The royal emblem of Laos and the national flag show a three-headed elephant called the *erawan*.

During the rainy season many highways become muddy.   AID

The people of Laos are closely related to the Thais. Although they speak their own language, a Laotian can understand and be understood by a Thai. Until the French forced Thailand to give up the territory, Laos was a part of that country. During its history, Laos has been invaded by many people, including Chinese, Thais, Khmers, and finally the French, who gained control in 1888.

From 1888 until 1949, Laos was a part of French Indochina. In that year the French granted full independence, and Laos became a constitutional monarchy. There are two capitals, the only cities in Laos. Luang Prabang is the royal capital; Vientiane, with a population of 100,000, is the administrative, or business, capital.

Buddhism has been the religion of the people for many centuries. Luang Prabang, one of the two main cities we mentioned, is named for a statue of Buddha called the Prabang. It had been sent by a king of Ceylon to a Khmer king in Cambodia. The king of Laos at that time was married to a Khmer princess, and so the famous statue came to Laos.

There are Buddhist temples in every village. Vientiane, one of the capitals of Laos, is known as the City of a Thousand Temples. The temples are not as large or beautiful as those in Bangkok, but some of them are famous Buddhist shrines.

There have been several changes in government during the last few years. The politicians and army are divided among pro-Communists, anti-Communists, and neutralists. The neutralists do not want to be allied with either the Communists or the free world. Laos has become important because almost two-thirds is now under Communist control. The Communists use Laos as a training ground for their soldiers. Also, Communist soldiers from North Vietnam cross through the wild jungles of Laos in order to reach South Vietnam. This jungle road is called the Ho Chi Minh Trail. It is now frequently bombed by American planes.

Sunset on the Mekong River, most important river of Cambodia and Laos.

The map shows that the Mekong River forms a long boundary between Laos and Thailand. In the north, Laos has a short boundary with Cambodia. All the eastern boundary is with North Vietnam and South Vietnam.

Laos is landlocked, and the nearest port city is Bangkok. The distance from Vientiane to Bangkok is 300 miles. Even though the country has received much American aid, the help does not seem to have changed the country. Some highways have been built, and Vientiane has some paved streets. But many people, especially the primitive tribespeople who live in the mountains, live as they did hundreds of years ago.

As we have said, Laos is important because it has become a battleground between the free world and the Communists. And most of the soldiers and supplies that reach the Vietcong in South Vietnam pass through Laos over the Ho Chi Minh Trail. We hope this interesting little country can remain free. But its future probably depends on what happens in the war in Vietnam. Now let's read about Vietnam, or rather the two Vietnams, north and south.

The "Chinese" Nations

NORTH AND SOUTH VIETNAM*

There is a mountain range near the border of Cambodia and Vietnam. On the western, or Cambodian, side, people eat with their fingers, as is done in India. On the eastern, or Vietnamese, side of the mountains, people eat with chopsticks. As we know, this is the way the Chinese eat. This mountain range illustrates how Southeast Asia is divided into people whose way of life has been influenced by India and people who follow a more Chinese way of life.

We should not suppose that there are no Buddhists in Vietnam. There are many Buddhists. Our newspapers have carried stories about the Buddhist monks in Saigon who burned themselves to death. But the Buddhism of Vietnam came from China, and it is different from that of Thailand, Cambodia, and Laos.

As we have read about Southeast Asia, we have learned that there are many Chinese in each country. But these Chinese emigrated to Southeast Asia in modern times. We call North and South Vietnam "Chinese" nations because the Vietnamese came from South China hundreds of years ago. And at various times, beginning before the time of Christ, Vietnam was ruled by China. The early history of Vietnam is closely related to the history of China.

The word "Vietnam" is quite new. Centuries ago this part of Southeast Asia, generally called the Indochinese Peninsula, was divided into three parts. Tongking lay just south of the border of China. Annam extended along the coast from near the city of Hanoi. The part of the peninsula around the delta of the Mekong River was called Cochin China.

*For a complete story of Vietnam, see John C. Caldwell, *Let's Visit Vietnam* (New York, The John Day Co., 1966).

The original inhabitants of Vietnam were mountain tribespeople like these.

There were numerous tribespeople living in the area we now call Vietnam, but the Vietnamese, as they prefer to be called, are now the most numerous people on the peninsula. After they pushed down the coast from China, some intermarried with the tribespeople. But for the most part the tribes were pushed into the mountains, where they still live.

It would take a whole book just to tell about the history of Vietnam. Altogether there were sixteen dynasties, or lines of kings. There were kings of Annam and kings of Tongking. For centuries there were wars between the various sections of Vietnam and Chinese invasions from the north. Then the French decided they wanted a big colony in the Far East.

The French defeated the Vietnamese in the Battle of Chihoa in 1861. This resulted in the capture of Saigon. During the next twenty years France slowly gobbled up the rest of Vietnam. We have read that France forced Thailand to give up Laos in 1888. By 1895 all parts of Vietnam were under French control. The big French colony was divided into three parts — Cambodia, Laos, and the three sections of Vietnam. Each nation was allowed to keep its kings, who had no power at all. The French established Saigon as the headquarters for their government.

The French developed rubber plantations and built a few highways and railroads. Both Saigon and Hanoi became large and modern cities. But the French did not give the people an opportunity to have a part in the government. The few people who were educated learned to speak French. This is still the second language of Vietnam, Cambodia, and Laos.

The people of Indochina, as the colony was called, never liked the French. They never gave up the idea of becoming free and independent. During World War II most of the colony was occupied by the Japanese. Many Vietnamese became guerrilla fighters. A Communist leader named Ho Chi Minh was able to capture much of Tongking. Just after the end of the war, Ho's guerilla armies were able to seize the big northern city of Hanoi.

Ho Chi Minh and other leaders wanted independence, but they were willing to give France time to train people in government. The French, however, would not consider independence under any terms. This resulted in full-scale war, which began in late 1946.

Called the Indochinese War, the fighting lasted for seven years and seven months. Although there was some fighting in Laos and Cambodia, most of the war was in Vietnam. Ho Chi Minh, the Communist, became the leader of the Vietnamese guerrillas. These Communist armies called themselves the Vietminh, and with help from Communist China and Russia, they defeated the French. The last great battle took place at Dienbienphu, which was surrendered by the French after a fifty-day siege.

France lost 253,000 men in the Indochinese War; the

Vietminh, about 200,000. In the Battle of Dienbienphu the French had 16,000 men. Of these, 6,000 were killed or wounded and 10,000 were captured. The war cost France $5,000,000,000.

The war ended in 1954. As a result of the peace treaty and other agreements made in Geneva, Switzerland, Vietnam was divided into two parts at the seventeenth parallel of latitude. The northern part became an independent Communist nation under the leadership of Ho Chi Minh. The southern part became a free and independent republic.

It was in this way that we now have two Vietnams. The total area of the two Vietnams is 127,380 square miles. North Vietnam covers about 61,000 square miles and has a population of more than 17,000,000. Hanoi, a city of 650,000 persons, is the capital.

South Vietnam is somewhat larger, with an area of 66,000 square miles and a population of about 16,000,000. Saigon, a city of more than 2,000,000 persons, is the capital.

Foreign visitors are not welcomed in Communist North Vietnam. We do know that the Communists are ruling the people harshly. There is no freedom of speech or religion. The many thousands of Catholics have been persecuted. Almost 1,000,000 Vietnamese have left North Vietnam to live in the south. Perhaps this figure shows us that the Communist government has not been popular.

Since the people of North and South Vietnam are alike, with the same general customs, we shall learn about them by reading about the people of South Vietnam. This country has become of great importance to the United States. As this book is being written, there are more than 300,000 American soldiers, sailors, and airmen in South Vietnam. It is estimated that should the war continue, there will be 500,000 American men in South Vietnam by late 1967.

All Vietnam lies within the tropics. The climate, like that of Thailand and Cambodia, is hot. There is a rainy, or monsoon, season through the late spring and summer, and a dry season in the fall and winter. The country is rich in rubber, tin, zinc, iron, and coal. There is a rice surplus. This means that the farmers grow more rice than the people need. This

Vietnamese farmer harvesting rice.

AID

is one of the reasons Vietnam is an important country. Nearly all the people of Asia eat rice. But many countries do not produce as much as they need.

Most of the Vietnamese live in the flat areas along the coast of the South China Sea or in river valleys. There is a big flat area where the Mekong River empties into the sea. This is one of the richest rice-producing areas in the world. Rice is also grown in other river valleys. There are many brush- or jungle-covered hills and many mountain ranges. If you were to fly over Vietnam in a plane, you could look down and see range after range of jungle-covered mountains.

The Vietcong hide in the mountains or in the swamps in the Mekong Delta. In some places they have dug miles of

Pumping water into rice fields by foot power.   AID

tunnels and can almost live underground. It is easy then to sneak out at night to attack villages or to set up ambushes.

As we have said, the Vietnamese live along the coast and in the river valleys. Tribespeople called the Montagnards (pronounced mone-tan-YARDS) live deep in the jungles or in the mountains. From our visits to other Southeast Asian countries, you can probably guess that there is also one other people found in Vietnam — the Chinese. There are almost 2,000,000 of them, for wherever there is trade and business, there are Chinese.

There are three different dialects spoken in the north, central, and southern parts of Vietnam. The language is, like the Thai and Chinese languages, tonal. We know that this means that each word can have different meanings depending on the tone of pronunciation. Although all its neighbors have had written languages for centuries, the Vietnamese had no way of writing until the missionaries invented a system. The language uses the letters of our alphabet and is phonetic. This means that words are written just as they sound. Many educated Vietnamese speak French. And many people have learned to speak English in the past few years.

In their liking for food, Vietnamese are much like Chinese. Everyone eats rice, and everyone likes to drink tea. Pork and fish are important parts of the diet. There are several kinds of very hot and very smelly sauces that are eaten with rice, fish, or meat.

Saigon, the capital city, lies on a small river. But it is close enough to the sea for large ships to reach. The city is divided into two parts: Saigon proper and Cholon, where more than 500,000 Chinese live. Saigon is a modern city with many broad streets filled with automobiles, bicycles, and pedicabs. This is a kind of rickshaw found throughout Southeast Asia. In Vietnam and Cambodia, pedicabs have bicycles attached behind the cab where people sit. The driver pushes rather than pulls. In other parts of Southeast Asia the bicycle is sometimes in front, sometimes on the side of the cab.

Saigon and Hanoi and Haiphong in North Vietnam are modern cities, but most Vietnamese live on farms or in villages. The French built few schools and trained very few

This is a Vietnamese pedicab, called a dustbin.   USIS

doctors. There are many people who cannot read or write; disease is a constant problem. And we must remember that there has been war in Vietnam since 1946. Many young Vietnamese cannot remember any time in their lives when there was peace. The war has taken many lives and not only of soldiers. The Vietcong, as we call the Communists in South Vietnam, have murdered or kidnapped thousands of people. Farmers have had their crops taken from them. Schools and churches have been destroyed.

Vietnam could be a prosperous land. Like Thailand, it can produce more rice than is needed. Before the fighting started, Vietnam was the fourth largest producer of natural rubber. But after years of fighting, the rubber plantations have been largely destroyed. The Vietcong control many roads and keep the farmers from selling their rice. There are many refugees, some of whom must live on a few cents a day.

We could say that the Vietnamese have been a quarrelsome people throughout their history. During the past few years the South Vietnamese have fought not only the Communists, but also one another. Northerners often do not like southerners. Buddhists and Catholics have often fought and quarreled. Because of French missionary work years ago, there are more than 1,000,000 Catholics. Most other Vietnamese belong to one of the many Buddhist sects. In other Buddhist nations a place of worship is called a temple or shrine. In Vietnam, Buddhist places of worship are called pagodas.

During the past few years Southeast Asia has become very important to the United States. Our country is pledged to defend Thailand. We have promised to help the Vietnamese free their country from Communist threats. Every day Americans are being killed in the battle against the Vietcong. Every day scores of American war planes bomb military targets in North Vietnam. The United States is spending billions of dollars to help South Vietnam remain free and become strong. While fighting the Communists, our government has also constantly tried to arrange a peaceful solution to the war. Unfortunately, the North Vietnamese government seems to prefer to fight.

The war in Vietnam may last several years. And even when the fighting ends, there will be need for American help. Only though American economic aid can the South Vietnamese rebuild their war-torn country.

If the people of Southeast Asia can be free of war and the threats of war, they can be prosperous. Our President has suggested that with our help all the nations along the Mekong River could work together to harness the river. There could be dams to produce electric power and irrigation water during the dry seasons. With electricity, there could be more and more factories and industry. With more and better jobs, people could become educated. Problems of health and poverty could be solved.

We hope the fighting will soon end. Then, instead of soldiers, the United States could send Peace Corps workers to all the nations of Southeast Asia.

Index

aborigine, 13
Angkor, 75
Angkor Wat, 76
Annam, 85, 87
Arabs, 15-17, 34
Ayut'ia, 67

Bali, 59
Bangkok, 68, 71, 84
Bangkok Dynasty, 68
Borneo, 37, 38, 44
British, 35, 36, 44, 56
Brooke, James, 44-45
Brunei, 45, 49
Buddha, 64
Buddhism, 15, 17, 22, 82, 94
Buddhist nations, 64-84
Buddhists, 85

Cambodia, 22, 75-80
Chinese, 22-29, 37, 41, 50-51, 60, 72, 85
Chunlalongkorn, 68
Cochin China, 85
Columbus, 58
Communism, 62
Communist China, 9, 29
Communists, 83, 89, 94

Dienbienphu, 88
Dutch, 19, 20, 35, 58, 60-62
Dyaks, 46, 47

East India Company, 19, 36, 59

Faber, Mount, 55
Federation of Malaysia, 20, 33-38, 54
French, 20, 33-38, 54, 77-78, 79, 82, 88, 87, 93

Gautama, 64
Geneva Treaty, 89
George Town, 43
Great Britain, 20, 25, 35, 50

Haiphong, 93
Hanoi, 85, 89, 93
Hinduism, 15
Hindus, 59
Ho Chi Minh, 88
Ho Chi Minh Trail, 83, 84
Hong Kong, 19, 21, 24, 25-33

Indochina, 88
Indonesia, 8, 21, 55, 56-64
Islam, 16

Jakarta, 11, 59
Java, 57, 59

Kalimantan, 59
Khmers, 75, 77, 82
Kinabulu, Mount, 37

Kra Isthmus, 11
Kuala Lumpur, 43

Laos, 8, 22, 81-84
Leonowens, Mrs. Anna, 68
Luang Prabang, 82

Majapahit, 58
Malacca, 15, 34, 35, 39
Malay, 33, 34, 37, 39, 50, 53
Malaya, 19, 21, 33, 34, 35, 38-44
Malay Peninsula, 10, 11, 12, 14, 15, 16, 17, 21, 36, 37, 38
Malaysia, 8, 9, 22, 33, 49-51
Mekong River, 79, 84, 85, 91
Melanesians, 14
Mohammedanism, 16
Moluccas, 60
Mongkut, 68
Montagnards, 92
Moslems, 34, 58

oil, 10
Oong Nai-siong, 46

pedicab, 23, 72, 93
Penang, 36, 39
Polynesians, 14
Portuguese, 19-20, 35

Raffles, Sir Stamford, 35, 52-53
Rama IV, King, 68
Rama V, King, 68-69
rice, 8-9, 23, 43, 94
rubber, 9, 39-41

Sabah, 37, 44-49
Saigon, 8, 87, 93
Sarawak, 44-49
SEATO, 8, 74
Siam, 20, 22, 69
Singapore, 8, 11, 22, 35, 36, 37, 38, 51-56
Southeast Asia
 chart of countries, 24
 history, 13-20
 transportation, 23
 weather, 12-13, 22
spices, 10, 17, 18, 42
Straits Settlements, 36, 53
Sukhut'ai, 67
Sulawesi, 60

Thailand, 8, 9, 12, 20, 22, 38, 64-75
tin, 9, 39, 41-42
Tongking, 85, 87

United East India Company, 19

Vietcong, 91, 95
Vietminh, 88-89
Vietnam, 8, 9, 22, 84-95